SMOKING MEAT PORK PROJECT

Complete Smoker Cookbook for Real Pork Lovers, The Ultimate How-To Guide for Smoking Pork

BY DEAN WOODS

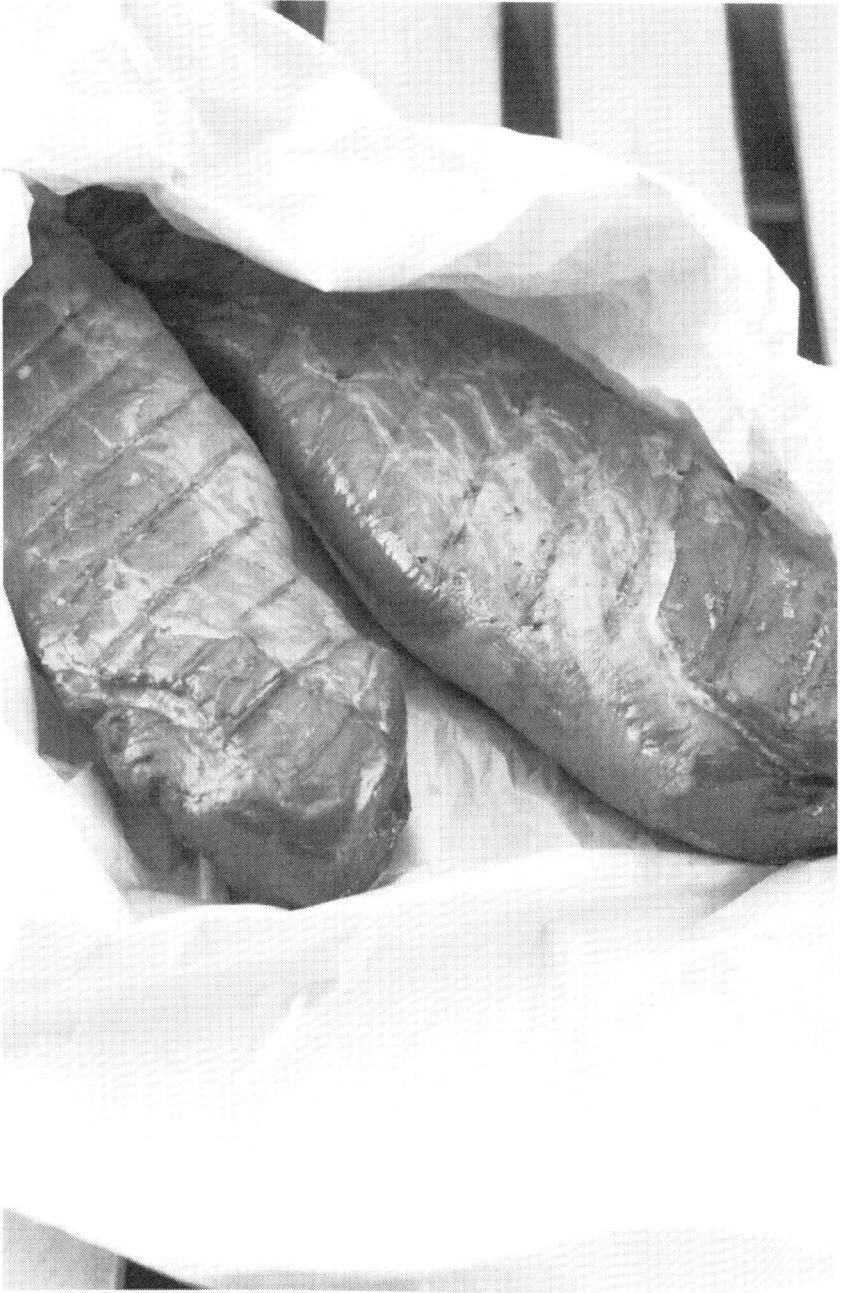

TABLE OF CONTENTS

Why Smoking...................................7

The Recipes..................................9

  Apple Injected Smoked Pork.................9

  Smoked Ribs With Dry Rub 11

  Smoked Boston Pork Butt.................14

  Tea-Smoked Pork Butt....................16

  Smoked Pork Ribs........................19

  Smoked Pork Bacon.......................22

  Grilled Smoked Pork Chops...............24

  Smoked Pork Kyle Style 26

  Slow Smoked Pork Shoulder 30

  Smoked Pork Chops With Corn & Okra 33

  Grilled Jerk Rack Of Pork 35

  Smoked Pork Tenderloin..................38

  Smoked Pork & Tender Cabbage Stir-Fry 43

  Fennel-Garlic Smoked Pork...............46

  Smoked Gouda with Bacon.................50

Spice Rubbed Smoked Ribs *53*

Smoked Pork Shoulder *56*

Smoked Glazed Spare Ribs............................*59*

Smoked Pork Loin with Rasberry Chipotle Glaze

....*61*

Smoked Legs of Suckling Pig............................*63*

Cold Smoked Pork Chops *67*

Smoked Pork Chops with Bleu Cheese.............*70*

Braised Collard Greens With Smoked Pork.......*75*

Vietnamese Grilled Smoked Pork....................*77*

Information about Smoking Meat.....*80*

Difference between cold and hot smoking.......*80*

The different types of Smokers *82*

The different styles of smokers.........................*84*

Choose your wood...*85*

The different types of Charcoal.......................*86*

Find the right temperature *87*

Cleanliness of the meat *88*

Keeping your meat cold..................................*90*

Keeping your meat covered............................*91*

Tools and Equipment...*92*

A note on curing meat.....................................*94*

Conclusion **96**

WHY SMOKING

Smoking is generally used as one of the cooking methods nowadays. The food enriches in protein such as meat would spoil quickly, if cooked for a longer period of time with modern cooking techniques. Whereas, Smoking is a low & slow process of cooking the meat. Where there is a smoke, there is a flavor. With white smoke, you can boost the flavor of your food. In addition to this statement, you can preserve the nutrition present in the food as well. This is flexible & one of the oldest techniques of making food. It's essential for you to brush the marinade over your food while you cook and let the miracle happen. The only thing you need to do is to add a handful of fresh coals or wood chips as and when required. Just taste your regular grilled meat and a smoked meat, you yourself would find the difference. Remember one thing i.e. "Smoking is an art". With a little time & practice, even you can become an expert. Once you become an expert with smoking technique, believe me, you would never look for other cooking techniques. To find one which smoking technique works for you, you must experiment with different woods & cooking methods. Just cook the meat over indirect heat source & cook it for hours. When smoking your meats, it's very important that you let the smoke to escape & move around.

THE RECIPES

APPLE INJECTED SMOKED PORK

TOTAL PREPARATION & COOKING TIME: 8
HOURS & 15 MINUTES
TOTAL SERVINGS: 12

INGREDIENTS

- 2 tbsp. Neely's Rub Seasoning, Dry
- 1 pork butt (6-8 pounds)
- 2 cups apple cider
- ¼ cup orange juice
- 2 tbsp. apple cider vinegar

- ½ tsp. cayenne pepper
- 2 tbsp. honey
- ½ cup lemon juice
- 2 tsp. kosher salt
- A dash of Worcestershire sauce

COOKING DIRECTIONS

1. Whisk the entire marinade ingredients together in a large-sized bowl.

2. Fill a large syringe with marinade & place the pork butt in a large-sized casserole dish. Inject ¾ of the marinade mixture into the pork using the syringe, preferably in several places. Transfer the leftover marinade on top of the pork. Using a plastic wrap; cover & let refrigerate until flavors permeate, for 2 to 12 hours.

3. Preheat your grill grate to 275 F on indirect heat in advance & add in the soaked apple-wood chips.

4. Drain any excess liquid from meat & place them on a paper towel; pat them dry. Season the pork with Rub seasoning to taste; ensure you cover the sides of the meat as well.

5. Arrange the coated pork butt (the preferably fat side facing up) on the grill. Grill for 6 hours, until tender. Transfer to a large-sized serving platter. Serve & enjoy.

SMOKED RIBS WITH DRY RUB

TOTAL PREPARATION & COOKING TIME: 3 HOURS & 30 MINUTES

TOTAL SERVINGS: 8

INGREDIENTS

For Ribs

- 4 slabs of baby back pork ribs (approximately 2 pounds each)
- Juice of 2 lemons, freshly squeezed
- ¾ cup white vinegar, distilled

For Rub

- ½ cup oregano, dried
- 1 cup smoked paprika
- ¾ cup Ancho Chile powder
- ½ cup celery seeds, toasted
- ¾ cup garlic powder
- ½ cup chili powder
- Freshly ground pepper & kosher salt to taste

OTHER INGREDIENTS

- Apple-wood, soaked in water for 15 minutes & drained

COOKING DIRECTIONS

1. Set up a grill over medium heat settings on indirect cooking; leaving one side of your grill without any heat source. Place the drained chips directly over the coals, if using a charcoal grill or put them inside a smoker box, if using a gas grill; placing them on top of the heat source.

2. *For Rub*: Thoroughly mix the garlic powder together with oregano, 2 tbsp. of pepper, celery seeds, ancho chile powder, chili powder, paprika & ¼ cup of salt in a large-sized bowl; mix well. Set approximately 1/3 of the mixture aside.

3. Now, prepare the ribs: In a spritzer bottle; combine lemon juice together with ¼ cup of water & vinegar. You need to baste the meat with this mixture during the cooking process.

4. Rub all of the ribs completely with the leftover dry rub and arrange them on the grill, preferably on the cooler side. Cover & cook for 2 and ½ hours; don't forget to spray the ribs with the lemon juice/vinegar mixture twice or thrice during the cooking process. When done, give the ribs the last spray & liberally sprinkle the kept aside dry rub until all sides of the meat are evenly coated.

SMOKED BOSTON PORK BUTT

TOTAL PREPARATION & COOKING TIME: 18
HOURS & 20 MINUTES

TOTAL SERVINGS: 6

INGREDIENTS

- 1 Boston pork butt (7-8 pounds)
- 4 ounces spice rub
- 1 cup apple cider or juice
- 2 tbsp. yellow mustard

COOKING DIRECTIONS

1. Preheat your smoker to 225 to 250 F in advance and rub mustard on all sides of the meat until evenly coated.

2. Now, apply the spice rub over the meat; make sure it's coated completely & create a paste.

3. Place the coated pork butt over the preheated smoker, preferably the fat-side up & smoke until a meat thermometer reflects the internal temperature of the meat to somewhere between 190 or 200 F; for 10 hours & 30 minutes.

4. It's important for you to leave the smoker closed for the initial 2 hours during the smoking process, and then spray a small quantity of apple cider or juice over the pork after every 2 hours.

5. Remove the cooked pork butt from smoker & before pulling it apart, let it rest for a minimum period of 15 minutes.

TEA-SMOKED PORK BUTT

TOTAL PREPARATION & COOKING TIME: 8
HOURS & 15 MINUTES

TOTAL SERVINGS: 8

INGREDIENTS

- 1 pork butt or shoulder (approximately 4 lbs.)

For Rub

- 1 tsp. Oregano, dried
- 2 tbsp. Brown sugar
- 1 tbsp. Hot paprika
- 1 tsp. Ground cumin
- 2 tsp. Garlic powder
- 1 tsp. Ground black pepper
- 1 tbsp. Kosher salt

For Wet Mop

- 8 potato roll buns
- 1 cup apple juice
- 3 tbsp. Yellow mustard
- 1 cup cider vinegar
- Oil, as required
- 1 tsp. Red pepper flakes

Others

- Hickory chips, soaked

COOKING DIRECTIONS

For Rub

- Stir brown sugar together with garlic powder, paprika, oregano, cumin, black pepper & salt in a small-sized bowl. Now, rub this mixture all over the pork butt until coated completely; let sit for a couple of hours at room temperature.

For Wet Mop

1. In the meantime, whisk vinegar together with apple juice, pepper flakes & mustard with a cup of water in a medium-sized bowl; whisk well. Cover & store until ready to use (preferably in a refrigerator).

2. Now, prepare a grill over indirect low heat settings and add in the wood chips on the direct side of your burner element: For the charcoal grill, bank a chimney starter (full of ash & lit) on top of the charcoal briquettes to one side of the grill. To avoid the flare-ups; don't forget to set up a drip pan on the other side.

3. Lightly coat the grill grates with oil. Cook the coated pork butt over indirect heat settings for 5 hours & 30 minutes, try to keep the temperature of the grill at approximately 225 F. Continue cooking for 2 to 4 & ½ hours more until a meat thermometer reflects 195 F when inserted into the thickest part of the meat. It's really important for you to baste the pork butt with the wet mop after every 15 to 20 minutes. Now, transfer the cooked pork butt to an aluminum pan, loosely tent with a foil & let rest for 20 to 25 minutes. Shred the meat using two large forks & transfer the shredded meat to a large-sized bowl. To moisten the pork butt further, feel free to add drippings & any remaining mop sauce over the pulled meat.

4. Serve over buns & enjoy.

SMOKED PORK RIBS

TOTAL PREPARATION & COOKING TIME: 3
HOURS & 35 MINUTES
TOTAL SERVINGS: 4

INGREDIENTS

- 2 baby-back pork ribs rack

For Rub

- 1 tbsp. oregano
- 2 tsp. ground coriander seeds, toasted
- A pinch of kosher salt
- 2 tsp. smoked paprika
- 1 tbsp. garlic salt
- Juice of 1 lemon, freshly squeezed

For Glaze

- 1 clove garlic, minced
- 1 tbsp. honey
- ½ red onion, small & minced
- 1 tbsp. red wine vinegar
- 1 tsp. of each oregano & thyme, fresh

To Finish

- 1 tbsp. oregano, fresh
- Sea salt to taste
- 1 lemon; cut in half
- Drizzle of honey
- 1 tbsp. extra-virgin olive oil

Others

- Apple-wood chips

COOKING DIRECTIONS

1. Mix the entire rub ingredients together in a large bowl; mix well. Moisten the ribs first with the lemon juice & then rub the above mixture on all sides of the meat until evenly coated.

2. Arrange your smoker or grill over indirect heat (ensure that you don't put the ribs directly over the heat source). Add ½ pound of the apple wood chips & place the ribs on the coolest part of your grill, wrap them in an aluminum foil, make some incisions in the aluminum foil & smoke the ribs for an hour over low heat settings.

3. In the meantime, whisk the entire glaze ingredients together in a separate large-sized bowl; whisk well.

4. After an hour of smoking, pour 1/3 of the glaze mixture over the ribs & seal them tightly in the foil; ensure you don't tear it. Perform the same step with the leftover racks. Place the ribs again on the grill & cook for 30 more minutes, preferably meat-side down & try to maintain the low heat settings; checking the heat settings occasionally. After half an hour, flip the foil bundles & continue to cook.

5. Remove ribs from the grill after an hour of cooking and let rest for half an hour in the foil. In the meantime, increase the grill's heat to medium-high. Grill the lemon in half, preferably flesh-side down for 4 to 6 minutes, until slightly soft & nicely marked.

6. When done, remove the foil from the ribs & place them on the grill; cook for 3 to 4 more minutes, preferably meat-side down. Flip & cook for 2 more minutes. Remove the ribs from grill & garnish the cooked ribs with a little drizzle of honey, grilled lemon, extra-virgin olive oil, oregano & sea salt. Serve warm & enjoy.

SMOKED PORK BACON

TOTAL PREPARATION & COOKING TIME: 3
HOURS & 35 MINUTES

TOTAL SERVINGS: 4

INGREDIENTS

- 5 lbs. Pork belly, with skin; rinsed under cold running tap water & pat dry
- 2 tbsp. Smoked sweet paprika
- ¼ cup dark brown sugar, packed
- 2 tbsp. Red pepper flakes

- ¼ cup honey
- 2 tsp. Pink curing salt
- 1 tsp. Cumin seeds
- ¼ cup kosher salt

COOKING DIRECTIONS

1. Transfer the dried pork belly to a 2-gallon re-sealable plastic bag. Now, mix the red pepper flakes with pink salt, kosher salt, brown sugar, honey, cumin & paprika in a large-sized bowl & prepare the spice rub. Rub this mixture over the pork belly until all sides are evenly coated.

2. Seal the bag & let refrigerate for several days until the pork belly feels firm, flipping once or twice during a day.

3. Remove the meat from bag, thoroughly rinse & pat them dry. Refrigerate on a rack for two days, uncovered.

4. Using apple-wood chips; prepare your smoker as per the directions provided by the manufacturer; setting the temperature to 200 F. Place the pork belly on the smoker & smoke until a meat thermometer reflects the internal temperature as 150 F, when inserted into the thickest part of the meat, for 3 hours or little longer.

5. Get rid of the rind and then slice & cook to your preference. Wrap the cooked bacon in a plastic wrap & feel free to refrigerate it for up to 1 week.

GRILLED SMOKED PORK CHOPS

TOTAL PREPARATION & COOKING TIME: 50 MINUTES

TOTAL SERVINGS: 8

INGREDIENTS

- 8 pork chops, thinly cut (approximately 1/2" thick)
- 1 tsp. Red pepper flakes
- ¼ cup honey
- 1 tbsp. Vegetable oil, plus more for grilling
- Juice of 1 lime, freshly squeezed
- ¼ cup light brown sugar

Cooking Directions

1. Preheat your grill pan over medium-high heat settings.

2. Combine sugar together with the lime juice, honey, red pepper flakes & oil in a re-sealable plastic bag, preferably large-sized.

3. Place the pork chops in the bag; shake well & let marinate for a minimum period of 20 minutes.

4. Remove the pork meat from marinade & brush the grill lightly with the oil.

5. Place the marinated pork chops over the grill & cook for a couple of minutes, until you can see the grill marks on the meat.

6. To create the diamond grill marks; rotate the pork chops to 90 degrees & grill for a couple of more minutes. Flip & cook for 2 more minutes.

7. Remove the pork chops from grill and transfer them to a large-sized serving platter. Serve & enjoy.

SMOKED PORK KYLE STYLE

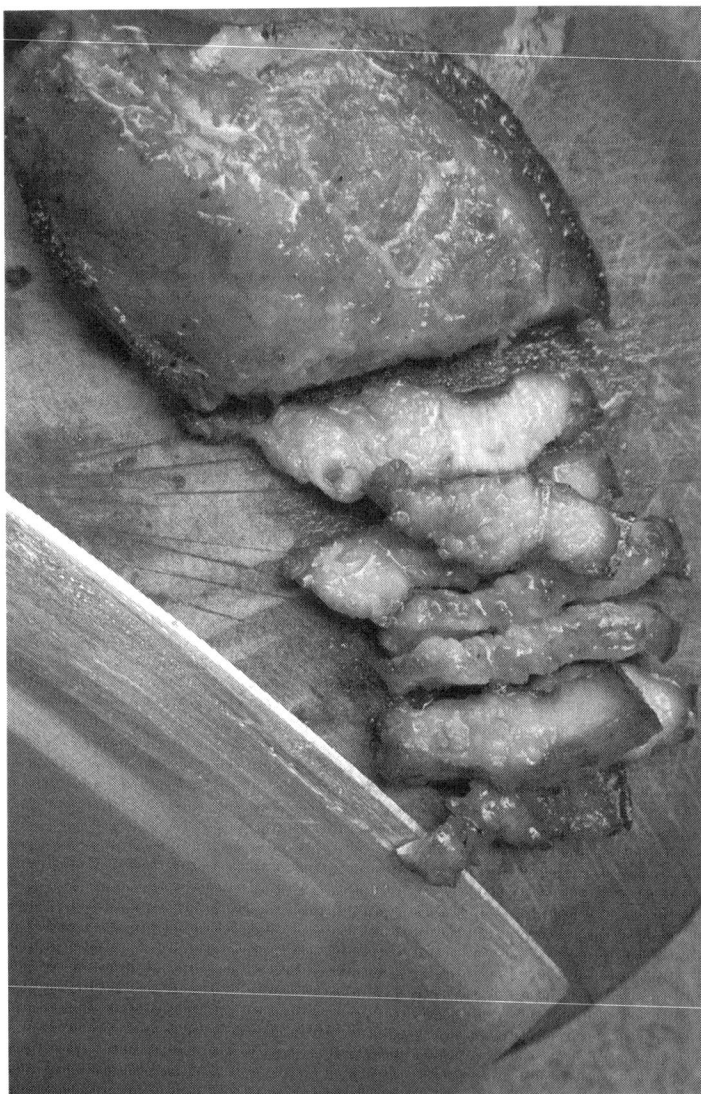

TOTAL PREPARATION & COOKING TIME: 12 HOURS & 30 MINUTES

TOTAL SERVINGS: 6

INGREDIENTS

- One pork butt (approximately 5 pounds)

For Glue

- 2 tbsp. yellow mustard
- Hickory & apple-wood chips, soaked in water for half an hour
- 1 tbsp. honey
- Charcoal, for smoker

For Rub

- 1 tbsp. Hickory salt
- ½ cup non-iodized salt
- 1 tbsp. Chili powder
- 1/3 cup black pepper
- 1 tbsp. Onion powder
- ¼ cup paprika
- 1 tbsp. Garlic powder
- 1 tsp. Ground cumin
- ¾ cup sugar
- 1 tbsp. Celery salt
- ¼ tsp. Cayenne pepper
- 1 tsp. Ground sage

For Marinade

- 1 chicken bouillon cube
- 1/8 cup Worcestershire sauce
- 2 cups cider vinegar
- 1/8 cup paprika
- 1 cup corn oil
- 1/8 cup white pepper
- 1 can of pineapple concentrate
- ¼ cup non-iodized salt

COOKING DIRECTIONS

For Marinade

- Dissolve the chicken bouillon cube in 2 tbsp. of water. Place the entire marinade ingredients together & Whisk in a large-sized bowl, preferably non-reactive.

For Glue

- Whisk the entire Glue ingredients together in a large bowl & place the mixture in a squeeze bottle.

For Rub

- Place the entire rub ingredients together in a container, preferably with lid; shake well.

For Pork

1. Set a cup of the marinade aside & inject a small amount of marinade into the meat in several places. Place the meat in a re-sealable plastic bag, preferably large-sized & cover with the leftover marinade. Let marinate in a refrigerator for several hours.

2. Remove the meat from marinade & then place them on paper towels; pat them dry.

3. To help the rub to stick; cover the pork with a very light coating of glue mixture. Generously sprinkle the rub; ensure you put the rub on the meat.

4. Prepare your smoker between 225 or 250 F & add in the hickory & apple chips to the charcoal lit.

5. Arrange the marinated pork butt on the smoker. Ensure you don't over-smoke the pork butt. Baste the pork with the kept aside marinade after 2 hours & place them again on the smoker for an hour more.

6. Baste again & place them in the smoker for an hour more. Repeat the basting process for one more time & smoke for an hour more.

7. Remove the pork butt from smoker & wrap them in aluminum foil; placing them on the smoker again until a meat thermometer reflects an internal temperature to 200 F.

8. When done, remove it from heat & let stand for 15 to 20 minutes before pulling or slicing.

Slow Smoked Pork Shoulder

Total Preparation & Cooking Time: 15 hours & 20 minutes
Total Servings: 8

INGREDIENTS

- One pork shoulder, boneless (approximately 5 pounds)
- 3 garlic cloves, chopped
- 2 tbsp. Light brown sugar
- Hot sauce
- 1 tsp. Ground coriander
- ¾ cup orange juice, freshly squeezed
- 2 heaping tablespoons ancho chile powder
- Warm corn tortillas
- 1 white onion, large & chopped
- 4 sprigs of thyme, fresh

- 1 or 2 chipotle in adobo, chopped finely
- Napa Cabbage Slaw
- ½ cup lime juice, freshly squeezed
- 2 tsp. Ground cumin
- Fresh cilantro leaves
- 2 tbsp. Canola oil
- 1 cup crumbled queso fresco

For Napa Cabbage Slaw

- 4 green onions, chopped coarsely
- ¼ cup apple cider vinegar
- 1 tsp. Celery seeds
- 2 tbsp. Canola oil
- ¼ cup mayonnaise
- Freshly ground pepper & kosher salt to taste

COOKING DIRECTIONS

For Napa Cabbage Slaw

1. Whisk vinegar together with mayonnaise, celery seeds and oil until completely smooth and then season with pepper and salt to taste. Whisk in the Serrano Chiles and green onions; whisk well.

2. Place the carrots and cabbage in a large-sized bowl. Add the dressing & queso fresco; give everything a good toss until evenly combined

For Pork Shoulders

1. Over medium heat settings in a small-sized saucepan; heat the oil. Once hot; add the onions, garlic, thyme, coriander, Ancho Chile powder, cumin, brown sugar, lime juice, orange juice, chipotle and 1/2 water; cook for a couple of minutes, until the sugar is completely dissolved.

2. Remove the pan from heat & let cool at room temperature. Place the pork in a large pan & pour on top of the marinade. Cover & refrigerate for overnight.

3. Remove the meat from a refrigerator at least half an hour before you plan to cook them.

4. Preheat your charcoal grill over indirect heat settings & Place the already soaked wood chips over the coals.

5. Place the marinated pork shoulders on the grill; cover & smoke until the grill temperature reaches 220 F. To continue the smoking process, feel free to add more of chips as required until the internal temperature of the meat reaches 140 F. Continue cooking for a couple of more hours; until a thermometer registers the temperature as 190 F. Let the pork shoulders to rest for half an hour.

6. Shred the pork using two large forks & serve in warm tortillas topped with Napa Cabbage Slaw, hot sauce, queso fresco and fresh cilantro leaves.

Smoked Pork Chops With Corn & Okra

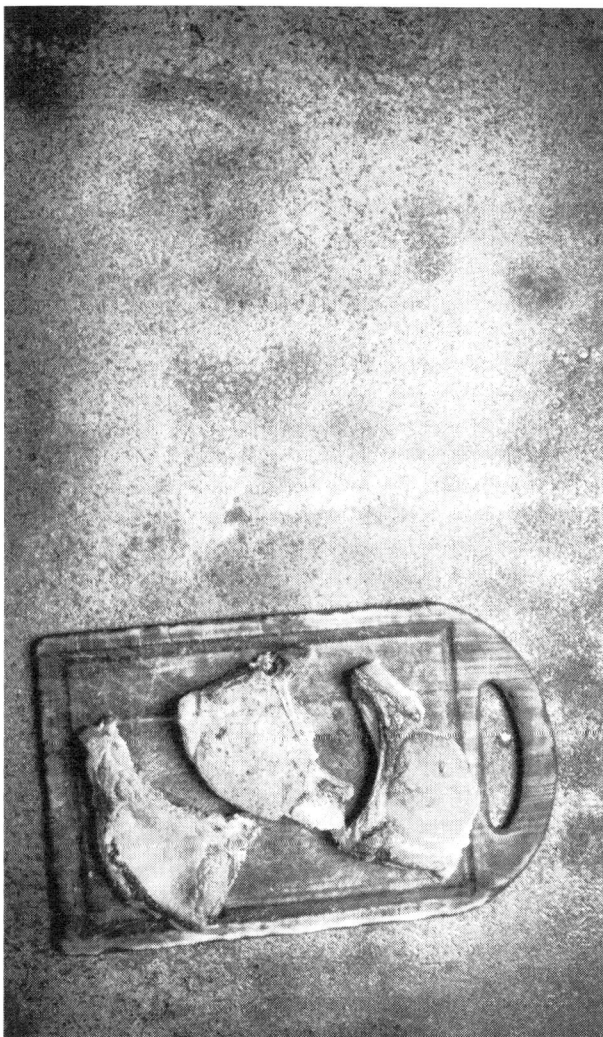

INGREDIENTS

- 4 bone-in pork chops, smoked (approximately ¾" thick) or 1 ¼ pounds ham steak, sliced into 4 even sized pieces
- 1 tbsp. vegetable oil
- 3 ears corn, shucked & kernels cut off
- 1 onion, small & chopped
- 1 tbsp. honey
- ¼ pound okra, sliced thinly
- 1 tomato, large & chopped
- ¼ tsp. Cajun seasoning, plus additional for sprinkling
- Freshly ground pepper to taste

COOKING DIRECTIONS

1. Sprinkle the meat with Cajun seasoning & pepper to taste. Over medium-high heat settings in a large skillet; heat the vegetable oil.

2. Once hot; cook the pork chops for 3 minutes on each side, until golden brown. Transfer the browned pork chops to a large-sized plate.

3. Add onion to the hot skillet & cook for 5 minutes, until softened.

4. Add the okra and corn; cook for 2 minutes, until tender-crisp.

5. Add the tomato, ¼ tsp. Cajun seasoning, honey & 3 tbsp. water; cook for a couple of minutes, until the tomato is softened slightly.

6. Place the chops again in the hot skillet; cover & cook for 2 to 5 minutes, until the chops are heated through & vegetables are tender.

GRILLED JERK RACK OF POR

TOTAL PREPARATION & COOKING TIME: 55 MINUTES

TOTAL SERVINGS: 8

INGREDIENTS

For Brine & Pork

- 10 allspice berries
- 1 rack of pork, center-cut, chine bone removed (approximately 3 pounds)
- 12 sprigs of thyme, fresh
- ½ cup brown sugar
- 8 whole cloves
- 1 head of garlic, sliced into ½
- 10 black peppercorns

- 4" ginger, fresh & chopped
- 2 bay leaves
- 1 Spanish onion, quartered
- 4 cinnamon sticks
- ½ cup kosher salt

For Spice Mixture

- 2 tbsp. ground coriander
- 1 tbsp. garlic powder
- 2 tbsp. ground ginger
- 1 tbsp. habanero powder
- 2 tbsp. light brown sugar
- 1 tbsp. onion powder
- 2 tsp. black pepper, coarsely ground
- 1 tsp. allspice
- 2 tsp. thyme, dried
- 1 tsp. cinnamon
- Canola oil, for brushing
- 1 tsp. ground cloves

COOKING DIRECTIONS

For brine & pork

1. In a large stockpot; bring 12 cups of water together with the peppercorns, allspice, brown sugar, salt, thyme, cloves, bay leaves, ginger, cinnamon sticks, onions, and garlic to a simmer; cook until the salt and sugar are completely dissolved. Set aside & let completely cool.

2. Place a plate on top & submerge the pork in the salted water. Using a plastic wrap; cover & let refrigerate for a minimum period of 12 hours or for up to 24 hours.

3. Remove the meat from brine, rinse under cold running tap water & pat them dry. Line the rack with the baking sheet and place the meat over it; let refrigerator for an hour. Remove the meat from the refrigerator at least half an hour before you plan to cook.

For Spice Mixture

1. In a small-sized bowl; thoroughly mix ginger with coriander, garlic powder, brown sugar, onion powder, habanero powder, black pepper, allspice, thyme, cloves & cinnamon; mix well. Brush the meat first with the canola oil and then rub the spice mixture on all sides.

2. Add hot charcoal to the ceramic cooker & place it on the grill rack.

3. When hot, place the pork & cook until charred slightly, preferably fat-side down.

4. Remove the grill rack & the pork, scatter the wood chips on top of the hot charcoal and then put on the ceramic plate & grill rack; place the pork (preferably seared-side up) again to the grill rack.

5. Close the cooker & try maintaining its internal temperature around 325 F. Cook the pork for 75 to 85 minutes, until a meat thermometer reflects 140 F. Before carving the meat into chops; let it rest for 10 minutes.

SMOKED PORK TENDERLOIN

TOTAL PREPARATION & COOKING TIME: 4
HOURS & 50 MINUTES
TOTAL SERVINGS: 8

INGREDIENTS

- 2 red bell peppers, large & roasted
- 24 ounces pork tenderloin, smoked
- 2 corn ears, roasted, cut from the cob
- 8 ounces pulled a pork butt
- 2 bacon strips, chopped
- 8 ounces wax beans, trimmed
- 4 wonton wrappers, large
- 8 ounces green beans, trimmed
- 2 ounces Vidalia onion, chopped
- 10 ounces Ancho Bourbon Sauce
- 2 baking russets potatoes, large, cooked & mashed
- 4 ounces water
- Pepper and salt to taste

For Smoked Pork Tenderloin

- 1-quart apple juice
- 1 tsp. clove
- 2 pork tenderloins
- 1 tsp. thyme
- 2 cups sugar
- 1 tsp. cinnamon
- 1 tbsp. black pepper
- 1 cup salt

For Pulled Pork Butt

- 1 pork butt, bone-in
- ½ cup spice

For Veal Jus

- 1 bay leaf
- 8 ounces onions, chopped
- 1-ounce cornstarch
- 4 ounces carrots, chopped
- 1 pound veal bones
- 4 ounces celery, chopped
- 1 tbsp. black peppercorns, cracked
- 1-quart veal stock
- 1 tbsp. vegetable oil
- 1 tbsp. water

For Ancho Bourbon Sauce

- 2 Ancho peppers
- ½ cup bacon, pepper-cured, diced
- 2 cups bourbon
- 1 onion, small & diced
- 2 tbsp. black pepper, freshly ground
- 1-quart veal jus
- 8 ounces brown sugar

COOKING DIRECTIONS

1. Thoroughly mix the pulled pork with peppers & corn over medium heat settings in a large saute pan. Stir & saute for a couple of minutes, until the mixture combines together. Season with pepper and salt to taste.

2. Lay the wonton wrapper flat & thinly spread the pulled pork mixture to ¼" from the edges. Arrange a smoked pork loin in the middle of the wrap. Fold the edges in & roll. Repeat this step for three more times. Set aside until you are ready to cook everything.

3. Render the bacon in a large-sized pan and caramelized onions with the bacon. Add beans & water only when the bacon is tender-crisp. Let simmer for several minutes, until tender.

4. In the meantime, preheat a fryer or a pot of oil to 360 F in advance.

5. Deep fry the wrap until warm throughout and crisp. Remove & place them on paper towels to drain. Cut on bias.

6. Place the mashed potatoes in the middle of the plate, position the sliced wrap over the potatoes & then place the beans and sauce in the middle.

For Veal Jus

- Heat the oil over moderate heat settings in a large stockpot. Add in the celery, carrots & onions; cook for a couple of minutes, until caramelized and then add in the veal bones, veal stock, peppercorns & bay leaf; bring everything together to a boil. Once boiling, decrease the heat settings & let simmer; cook for a minimum period of 2 & 1/2 hours, skimming any foam or fat off as required. For slurry; thoroughly mix the cornstarch with water in a small-sized bowl. Add the mixture to the jus & bring to a boil until thickened.

For Ancho Bourbon Sauce

- Render the bacon over moderate heat settings in a saucepan, preferably heavy-bottomed until turn golden brown. Now, cook the onions until caramelized, for a couple of minutes. Add the brown sugar & Ancho peppers; cook until the mixture starts bubbling. Carefully add the bourbon & immediately remove the pan from heat. Place the pan again to the heat & cook until you get a syrup-like consistency. Add the veal jus & black pepper; let simmer until you get your desired flavor and then strain.

For Smoked Pork Tenderloin

1. Thoroughly mix apple juice with cinnamon, pepper, clove, sugar, thyme & salt; give everything a good stir until the sugar and salt are dissolved completely. Add pork & brine, let refrigerate for several hours. Remove the meat from brine & dry in the refrigerator over a sheet pan on a rack for an hour.
2. Heat up your stovetop smoker with some apple wood chips. Smoke the pork tenderloin until cooked through.

For Pork Butt

1. Preheat your oven to 250 F in advance.

2. Trim any excess fat from the pork butt and then cut ¼" into the meat just like the criss-cross pattern. Coat the pork butt with the barbeque spice. Arrange the coated meat in a roasting pan attached to a rack; cover with a lid or foil. Cook until the internal temperature reaches 150 F.

3. Remove the pork butt from oven and let cool until easy to handle. Once cool, using your hands, shred the meat & remove any excess fat and bone.

Smoked Pork & Tender Cabbage Stir-Fry

TOTAL PREPARATION & COOKING TIME: 1 HOUR & 20 MINUTES

TOTAL SERVINGS: 4

INGREDIENTS

- 2 green onions, trimmed
- ½ pound pork butt, boneless
- 3 ginger slices, quarter-sized, peeled
- 4 cups water
- ¼ tsp. salt
- 2 tsp. sugar

For Smoking Mixture

- 1 ½ to 2 cups Napa cabbage, sliced (1")
- 3-star anise
- ¼ cup rice, uncooked
- 2 tsp. minced ginger
- ¼ cup light brown sugar, packed
- 2 tbsp. vegetable oil
- ¼ cup oolong or black tea leaves
- 2 tsp. green or red jalapeno chile, minced
- 1/3 cup carrot, sliced thinly
- 2 tsp. cornstarch, dissolved in 1 tbsp. of water
- 1/3 cup bamboo shoots, sliced
- 2 tbsp.soy sauce
- ¼ cup chicken stock
- 1 tbsp. garlic, minced
- 1 ½ tsp. garlic-chile sauce
- ¼ tsp. sesame oil

Cooking Directions

1. Place the pork butt in a saucepan (preferably 2-quart) and then add the water together with green onions, ginger, salt & sugar; bring everything together to a boil. Once boiling; decrease the heat settings & let simmer. Cover the pot & let simmer for 6 to 8 more minutes, until the meat is almost cooked through. Drain & set aside.

2. Line the wok's inside & its lid with an aluminum foil and prepare the smoking mixture. Stir rice together with the star anise, sugar and tea leaves in the lined wok and then evenly spread over the bottom. Place a round rack on top of the smoking mixture, approximately 3" above the mixture & place the meat in the middle.

3. Place the wok over high heat settings, uncovered. When the mixture starts to smoke; decrease the heat settings to medium & cover the wok; cook for half an hour or little less, until the meat turns into a rich & deep brown color. Turn the heat off & before removing the lid, let stand for 4 to 5 minutes.

4. Let the meat to briefly cool and then cut into slices, preferably 1/8" thick; discard the foil and smoking mixture. Clean the wok & heat the oil until very hot preferably over high heat settings; swirl to coat all sides of the wok. Cook the ginger, garlic & chile for half a minute, until fragrant, stirring frequently. Add in the carrot, pork, bamboo shoots, and cabbage; stir-fry for a minute, until the cabbage is wilted.

5. Add in the chile-garlic sauce, soy sauce & chicken stock; bring everything together to a boil. Once boiling; decrease the heat settings; cover the wok & let simmer for a couple of minutes, until the carrot is tender.

6. Add in the dissolved cornstarch; cook for half a minute more, until the sauce is slightly thickened, stirring frequently. Add the sesame oil; give everything a good stir, scoop onto a warm serving platter. Serve hot & enjoy.

Fennel-Garlic Smoked Pork

TOTAL PREPARATION & COOKING TIME: 1
HOUR & 20 MINUTES

TOTAL SERVINGS: 8

INGREDIENTS

For Smoked Pork

- 1 bone-in pork loin, center-cut (approximately 5 pounds), chine bone removed
- ¼ cup honey
- Freshly ground black pepper
- ½ cup balsamic vinegar
- Canola oil, for brushing

46

For Brine

- 2 heads of garlic, sliced crosswise
- ¼ cup Fennel seeds, toasted
- 1 small bunch of thyme sprigs, fresh
- ½ cup kosher salt
- A bunch of Fennel Fronds
- ¼ cup sugar

For Fennel Gremolata

- Juice and finely grated zest of 1 orange
- 1 Fennel bulb, small, plus fronds
- Grape Mostarda, for serving
- Extra-virgin olive oil

For Grape Mostarda

- 1 ½ pounds red Grapes, seedless, washed, dried & halved
- 2 tbsp. canola oil
- 1 tbsp. whole grain mustard
- ½ cup sugar
- 1 tbsp. yellow mustard seeds
- 2 shallots, diced finely
- ½ cup red wine vinegar
- 1 sprig of rosemary, fresh
- 2 tsp. orange zest, finely grated

COOKING DIRECTIONS

Fennel Gremolata

1. Fill a large saucepan with 8 cups of water and bring it to a boil over moderate heat settings. Add the sugar and salt; cook until completely

dissolved. Add the garlic, Fennel seeds, Fennel fronds, and thyme; remove from heat.

2. Set aside & let completely cool. Pour the brine into a large-sized plastic container and then add in the pork loin; cover & let refrigerate for an hour or for a couple of hours.

3. Remove the pork loin from brine, rinse well under cold running tap water & pat them dry. Put on a baking sheet on a rack & refrigerate for an hour or for over-night.

4. Remove the ceramic plate & grill grate from the cooker. Add the hot charcoal & scatter the soaked wood chips on the top. Place the ceramic plate & grill rack in the cooker Close the cover & bring the internal temperature to around 300 to 325 F and let smoke for 10 to 12 minutes.

5. Brush the loin completely with oil & then sprinkle pepper over the top. Place the coated pork loin on the rack, Close the cover & smoke for 1-1 hour & 30 minutes, until a meat thermometer reflects 140 F.

6. While you are smoking the pork, combine honey with balsamic vinegar. Start brushing the mixture over the pork. When completed; remove, loosely tent & let rest for 10 to 12 minutes before slicing.

7. Cut the Fennel into small-sized dice & chop the fronds coarsely; place them in a large bowl. Add the juice and zest & drizzle with a small amount of olive oil; mix until well combined. Let sit for a couple of minutes at room temperature.

8. Now, spoon the Grape Mostarda onto a large platter and top with the pork & spoon the Gremolata on top of the pork.

For Grape Mostarda

1. Overhigh heat settings in a large saucepan; heat the canola oil. Add the vinegar, Grapes, sugar, shallots, mustard seeds, ½ cup cold water, and rosemary. Bring everything together to a simmer; cook for 20 minutes, until the mixture thickens & the Grapes slightly soften, about 20 minutes.

2. Remove from heat & stir in the orange zest and mustard. Transfer everything together to a large bowl & set aside at room temperature to cool. Get rid of the rosemary sprig.

SMOKED GOUDA WITH BACON

TOTAL PREPARATION & COOKING TIME: 1 HOUR & 40 MINUTES

TOTAL SERVINGS: 8

Ingredients

- 6 bacon slices, thick cut
- 2 shallots, thinly sliced
- 1 pound asparagus
- 2 tbsp. extra-virgin olive oil
- 1 head cauliflower, cut into florets
- ¼ cup almonds, smoked, chopped coarsely
- 1 pound white mushrooms
- 1 ½ pounds kielbasa
- 2 red pears
- 1 cup baby Gherkin pickles or cornichons, drained
- 4 tsp. lemon juice, divided
- 1 garlic clove, large & smashed
- 8 ounces Gruyere, shredded
- 1/3 pound Gouda, smoked, shredded (approximately 6 ounces)
- 1 rounded tbsp. all-purpose flour
- 2 to 3 tablespoons red wine vinegar, eyeball it
- 1 baguette, sliced
- ¾ cup white wine, dry
- Salt and black pepper to taste

Cooking Directions

1. Fill a medium frying pan with approximately 2 or 3" water and heat until it starts boiling. Add salt & the cauliflower; cook for a couple of minutes, then using spider or tongs; remove from water to a colander. Let them cool under cold and running tap water.

2. Trim the tough ends from the asparagus and add them to the salted water; cook for a couple of minutes, remove & let cool in the same format as you did with the cauliflower. In the meantime;

51

over medium-high heat settings in a second skillet; heat 2 tbsp. of olive oil & saute the mushrooms and shallots for 8 to 10 minutes, until tender.

3. Season with pepper and salt; add red wine vinegar & cook for a minute. Remove the pan from heat.

4. Preheat your broiler over high heat settings & a large nonstick skillet or grill pan over medium-high heat settings. Drizzle extra-virgin olive oil over the sausage casing & using the tines of a fork, prick the skin in some Places. Grill the kielbasa in a large nonstick skillet or on a hot grill pan until the casing is crisp, for 6 to 8 minutes. Remove the sausage & cut them into chunks, preferably 2" on a bias.

5. While you are cooking the sausage, pile the veggies on a large-sized platter & add in the cornichons together with chopped pears coated with 2 tsp. of the lemon juice.

6. Broil the bacon until crisp on a slotted pan. Drain & let cool at room temperature and then chop. Now, mix the cheeses with flour in a large bowl. Rub smashed garlic inside a small pot & then discard.

7. Add wine & the leftover lemon juice; heat it up over medium heat until you can see bubbles. Decrease the heat settings & let simmer and then add the cheese.

8. Work in batches and continue to stir until the cheese melts. Using a large wooden spoon; stir in an eight-figure pattern. Transfer the fondue to fondue pot & top with smoked nuts and chopped bacon.

SPICE RUBBED SMOKED RIBS

TOTAL PREPARATION & COOKING TIME: 2
HOURS & 20 MINUTES
TOTAL SERVINGS: 8

INGREDIENTS

For Maple-Horseradish Glaze

- 2 heaping tbsp. Dijon mustard
- 1/2 cup prepared horseradish, drained
- 2 cups pure maple syrup
- 1 tbsp. Ancho chili powder
- Freshly ground pepper & salt to taste

For Ribs

- 3 tbsp. Ancho chili powder
- 4 pork ribs racks (3 lbs. each)
- 3 cups wood chips (hickory, mesquite, or applewood)
- 2 tbsp. ground coriander
- 1/3 cup Span ish paprika
- 2 tsp. ground black pepper
- 3 tbsp. New Mexican chili powder
- 1 tbsp. ground cumin
- 2 tbsp. kosher salt

COOKING DIRECTIONS

For Ribs

1. Stir the entire spices ingredients together in a medium-sized bowl.

2. Soak the hickory chips in water enough to cover the chips approximately ½ an hour before the cooking time; drain. Place slow burning charcoal in a covered grill, preferably on both sides of a drip pan. Sprinkle the coals with wood chips.

3. Rub the top side of each rib with approximately 3 tbsp. of rub.

4. Place the coated ribs on the grill, bone side down. Close the cover & grill for 1 & ½ hours, feel free to add more of chips after every 20 minutes.

5. Brush the meat liberally with Maple-Horseradish Glaze during the last 10 minutes of grilling.

For Glaze

- Whisk the entire glaze ingredients together in a medium-sized bowl. Season with pepper and salt, to taste.

SMOKED PORK SHOULDER

TOTAL PREPARATION & COOKING TIME: 6
HOURS & 20 MINUTES
TOTAL SERVINGS: 4

INGREDIENTS

- 10 pounds charcoal, hardwood & divided
- Peppery Vinegar Sauce
- 1 Boston butt pork roast or pork shoulder (5 to 6 pound)
- Cider Vinegar Barbecue Sauce
- 2 tsp. salt
- Hickory wood chunks

For Pepper Vinegar Sauce

- 1 tbsp. dried red pepper, crushed
- 1 ½ tsp. pepper
- 1-quart cider vinegar
- 1 tbsp. salt

For Cider Vinegar Sauce

- ½ tsp. onion powder
- 1 ½ cups cider vinegar
- ¼ cup ketchup
- 1 tbsp. hot sauce
- ½ tsp. Worcestershire sauce
- 1/3 cup brown sugar, firmly packed
- 1 tsp. browning & seasoning sauce
- ½ tsp. pepper & salt

COOKING DIRECTIONS

1. Sprinkle the pork generously with salt. Cover & let chill for half an hour.

2. Prepare your charcoal fire with approximately half of the charcoal in the grill. Allow it to burn until you can see some gray ash, for 15 to 20 minutes. Evenly push the coals on both sides of the grill. Place 2 hickory chunks carefully over each pile & arrange food rack over the grill.

3. Place the pork directly in the middle of the grill of your rack, preferably meat side down. Cover with lid, leaving the ventilation holes to remain open completely.

4. Prepare some more charcoal fire with approximately 12 briquettes in fire bucket or an auxiliary grill. Let burn until covered slightly with some gray ash, for half an hour.

5. Add 6 briquettes carefully to each pile in a smoker and add 2 hickory chunks more on each pile. Just repeat this step after every half an hour.

6. Continue cooking the pork until a meat thermometer reflects 165 F, for 5 hours & 30

minutes, covered. During the last 2 hours of cooking; turn the pork once.

7. Remove the pork from grill & let slightly cool at room temperature. Chop & serve with some of the Peppery Vinegar Sauce or Cider Vinegar Barbecue Sauce.

For Peppery Vinegar Sauce

• Stir the entire peppery sauce ingredients together in a large bowl, blend well.

For Cider Vinegar Sauce

• Stir the entire ingredients together in a medium-sized saucepan. Cover and cook until the sugar dissolves completely, for 7 minutes, over medium heat settings, stirring constantly. Cover & let the sauce to chill until ready to serve.

SMOKED GLAZED SPARE RIBS

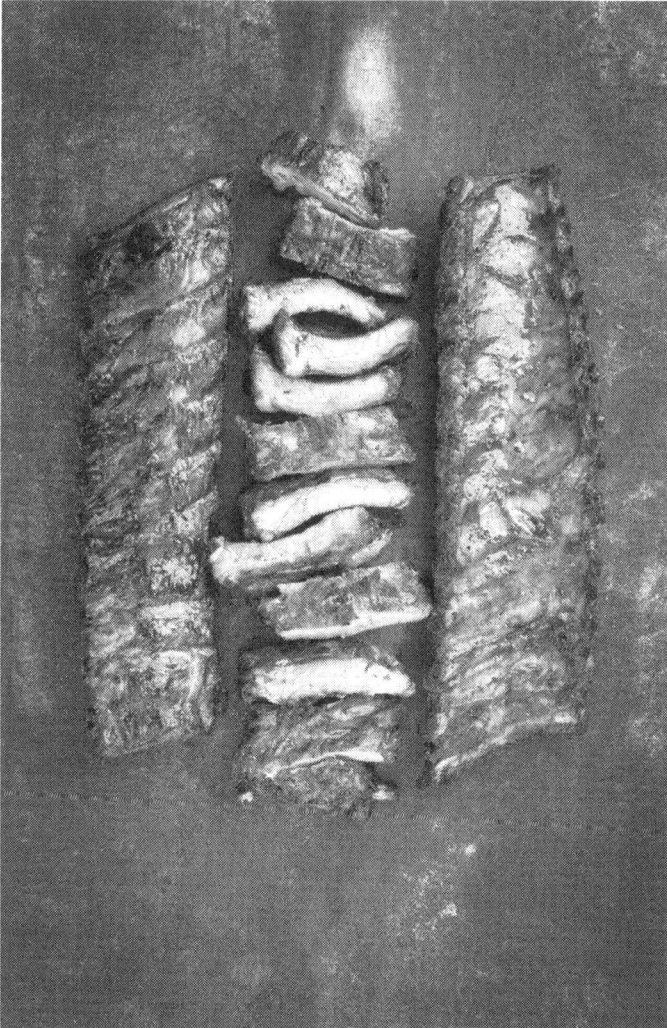

TOTAL PREPARATION & COOKING TIME: 4
HOURS & 20 MINUTES
TOTAL SERVINGS: 4

INGREDIENTS

- 1 tbsp. roasted Garlic pepper seasoning, preferably Irvine Spices
- 2 sides of pork spare ribs (approximately 3 pounds each)
- 1 tsp. garlic powder
- ½ cup honey
- 1 tsp. onion powder
- ½ cup brown sugar
- 1 tsp. lemon pepper
- 2 tsp. salt

COOKING DIRECTIONS

1. Rinse the spare ribs under cold running tap water & place them on paper towels; pat them dry. Combine the Garlic Pepper Seasoning together with lemon pepper, onion powder, salt and garlic powder in a small-sized bowl and prepare a rub. Rub the mixture over the spare ribs, preferably entire surface.

2. Preheat your smoker as per the directions provided by the manufacturer and try maintaining a temperature between 255 to 300 F (over indirect heat). Smoke the coated meat until cooked through.

3. Combine brown sugar together with honey in a small-sized bowl at the end of the smoking time & spread the mixture on the spare ribs.

SMOKED PORK LOIN WITH RASBERRY CHIPOTLE GLAZE

TOTAL PREPARATION & COOKING TIME: 2
HOURS & 10 MINUTES

TOTAL SERVINGS: 4

INGREDIENTS

- 1 jar raspberry jam, seedless (10 ounces)
- 1 pork loin (4 pounds); white silver skin trimmed
- 3 tbsp. spice rub, dry for pork
- 1 bottle Tabasco chipotle hot pepper sauce (5 ounces)
- Extra-virgin olive oil, as needed

COOKING DIRECTIONS

1. Preheat your outdoor smoker or stovetop to approximately 230 F in advance.

2. Coat the entire loin lightly with the olive oil. Liberally sprinkle the rub on the loin, preferably all sides.

3. Arrange the pork in smoker & smoke for an hour or two, until a meat thermometer reflects an internal temperature of pork as 150 F. Remove the pork from smoker & lightly wrap them in aluminum foil.

4. In the meantime, preheat your broiler.

5. Place the jam in a bowl, preferably medium-sized & stir in approximately 1/3 of the chipotle sauce; mix well, feel free to add more of chipotle sauce until you get your desired level of heat & taste.

6. Unwrap the pork & cover them with the glaze. Place the pork on a preheated broiler pan & broil for 3 minutes, until glaze starts bubbling. Slice the pork against the grain. Serve & enjoy.

SMOKED LEGS OF SUCKLING PIG

TOTAL PREPARATION & COOKING TIME: 16
HOURS & 10 MINUTES

TOTAL SERVINGS: 4

INGREDIENTS

- 2 hind quarters suckling pig, approximately 6 pounds each
- ½ cup molasses
- 1 tbsp. Five-spice powder
- Water, to cover
- 1 cup black tea leaves
- ¼ cup Chinese black vinegar
- 1 tbsp. ginger powder
- ½ cup dark soy sauce
- 1 cup rice
- 2 plus 1 cup sugar
- 1 cup salt

For Garlic-Bacon Grits

- ¼ cup scallions, sliced
- 6 bacon slices
- 1 jalapeno, minced
- 4 cups chicken stock
- 1 white onion, medium & minced
- 12 garlic cloves, sliced thinly
- 1 cup grits
- Salt and black pepper, to taste

For Cassia Apple Chutney

- 1 large yellow onion, 1/2-inch dice
- 2 tbsp. butter
- 1 cup apple juice
- ½ tbsp. cinnamon or cassia powder
- 8 Fuji apples, peeled & ½" dice
- 1/2 cup chopped chives, for garnish
- 1 heaping tbsp. ginger, minced
- 1 ¼ cups sambal
- White pepper & salt, to taste

COOKING DIRECTIONS

1. Place the legs in brine (salt, sugar & water mixture) for overnight. Using a large bamboo basket; prepare your steamer & cover.

2. Mix the molasses together with vinegar, soy, five-spice powder & ginger in a large-sized bowl. Coat the legs with the glaze & Place them in the steamer.

3. Steam for a couple of hours on low steam; don't forget to check the water level and brush the meat with more of glaze occasionally.

4. The meat is ready when you can easily penetrate the pork using a knife. Pull off the steamer basket with the pork, rub the glaze again & set aside.

5. Remove water from the wok, wipe it dry & line it with an aluminum foil.

6. Add the rice, sugar, and tea; mix well. Heat the wok over medium heat settings & watch for smoke.

7. When starts smoking, decrease the heat settings to low & place the basket again on the wok.

8. Using wet kitchen towels between the basket and wok; seal.

9. Smoke for 10 minutes on low heat settings. Turn on the wok over high heat settings for half a minute & then turn it off. It would continue to smoke & let stand for half an hour.

10. Just deep fry the pork.

For Cassia Apple Chutney

1. Over medium heat settings in a large saucepan, melt a tbsp. of butter & saute the onions and ginger for 3 to 4 minutes, until soft.

2. Add apples and cassia; cook for a couple of more minutes & season to taste. Add in the juice & let simmer until reduced by half. Whisk in the leftover butter & check the amount of seasoning.

3. Place the grits in middle on a large platter & surround them with apples. Place pig over the top & garnish with chives.

4. Serve on the side of sambal & enjoy.

For Garlic-Bacon Grits

1. Over medium heat settings in a large skillet, cook the bacon until crisp, for several minutes.

2. Place the cooked bacon on paper towels & drain; when cool, chop into pieces, preferably 1/8". Pour the bacon fat off & reserve. Add garlic, onions, and jalapeno in the same skillet, brown & season for 5 to 6 minutes.

3. Add the stock & let it boil. Slowly sprinkle the grits; Whisk until evenly incorporated. Cover & let simmer until all of the liquid is absorbed, for 12 minutes, preferably over very low heat settings. Check for seasoning & feel free to add back the scallions and bacon.

4. Serve hot & enjoy.

COLD SMOKED PORK CHOPS

TOTAL PREPARATION & COOKING TIME: 1
HOUR & 50 MINUTES
TOTAL SERVINGS: 4

INGREDIENTS

- 4 bone-in pork chops, center cut (1-inch)
- 1 ½ cups wood chips (mesquite or apple wood or hickory), soaked in cold water for half an hour
- Freshly ground black pepper & salt to taste
- 1 cup balsamic vinegar
- A pinch of all-spice
- ¼ cup maple syrup
- Canola oil

COOKING DIRECTIONS

1. Preheat your oven to 400 F in advance. Spread the wood chips evenly in the bottom of your roasting pan. Tightly cover the top with an aluminum foil. Place in the oven for 15 minutes, until the chips begin to smoke and get hot.

2. Remove the pan from oven & remove the foil from the pan as well. Place a baking rack inside the pan & arrange the chops on the rack, leaving couple inches of space among each one. Cover quickly with the foil & let sit for 10 to 15 minutes on your kitchen counter.

3. While you are smoking the pork chops, put the vinegar over high heat settings in a small pan & cook for a couple of minutes, until reduced to ¼ cup. Remove from heat & Whisk in the allspice, maple syrup, pepper and salt to taste. Let slightly cool at room temperature.

4. Heat a grill pan, preferably over medium-high heat settings. Using canola oil; lightly brush the ridges. Brush both sides of the chops with some of the glazes & then season with pepper and salt.

5. Grill both sides for 7 minutes per side, until slightly charred, golden brown & cooked to medium doneness, feel free to brush with more of glaze. Remove from grill, tent it loosely & let rest for a couple of more minutes. Transfer to a large-sized serving platter. Serve & enjoy.

SMOKED PORK CHOPS WITH BLEU CHEESE

TOTAL PREPARATION & COOKING TIME: 3
HOURS & 35 MINUTES
TOTAL SERVINGS: 4

INGREDIENTS

For Yukon Gold, Bleu Cheese & Garlic Mashed Potatoes

- 1 tbsp. garlic, chopped
- 2 pounds Yukon gold potatoes, cubed
- 1 cup milk
- Bleu cheese, to taste
- 1 cup chicken stock
- Pepper & salt to taste
- For Hickory-smoked Pork Chops:
- Baby portobello mushroom, steamed
- 1 tbsp. garlic, minced
- Onion Straws
- 2 cups milk
- Rosemary sprigs
- 3 pork chops, medium
- Caramelized Pears
- Roasted red pepper
- Yukon gold, blue cheese, and garlic mashed potatoes
- Pepper & salt to taste

For Caramelized Pears

- 4 tbsp. all-purpose flour
- 2 pears, sliced
- 1 clove garlic, chopped
- 4 tbsp. butter
- 1 cup apple juice concentrate

For Roasted Red Pepper

- 1 baby portobello mushroom, whole; thoroughly clean the skin

- Steamed Baby Portobello Mushroom:
- 1 red pepper, whole; thoroughly clean the skin
- Olive oil, for rubbing
- 1 clove garlic, chopped
- Salt and pepper

For Onion Straws

- All-purpose flour, for dredging
- 1/4 cup milk
- Olive oil, 2 tablespoons
- 1 Vidalia onion, sliced
- Vegetable oil, for frying
- Salt and pepper

COOKING DIRECTIONS

For Hickory-smoked Pork Chops

1. Combine milk together with garlic, rosemary, pepper, and salt in a medium-sized bowl. Place the pork chops inside the bowl & let marinate for half an hour.

2. Sear the pork chops, preferably each side over an open-flame grill, until you can see some black grill marks on them.

3. Remove the meat from the grill. Over medium-high heat settings in a large saute pan and Place the hickory smoking chips in the bottom.

4. Cover the grill with a lid and then place every pork chop over the lid. Smoke until the meat is fork tender. Serve with onion straws, pears, and potatoes. Garnish with mushroom and red pepper strips.

For Caramelized Pears

1. Combine the entire ingredients in a medium-sized saute pan, over medium heat & saute until the sauce thickens & the pears soften; set aside.

2. For Yukon Gold, Bleu Cheese & Garlic Mashed Potatoes:

3. Add potatoes in a large pot and then cover the pot with water (enough to cover the potatoes); bring to a rolling boil. Continue to boil until the potatoes are soft.

4. Place the boiled potatoes in a medium bowl & drain the water. Add the leftover ingredients to the bowl; mash until you get your desired creaminess; set aside.

For Onion Straws

1. Combine milk together with oil, pepper, and salt in a medium-sized bowl. Slice an onion into long strips & then Place them into milk mixture.

2. Shake any excess liquid off from the onion strips & then dredge them in the flour. Heat oil in a medium-sized sautes pan over medium-high heat settings.

3. Cook the dredged onions in the saute pan for a couple of minutes, until brown & crispy slightly; set aside.

4. For Steamed Baby Portobello Mushroom:

5. Rub the surface of the baby mushroom generously with olive oil, garlic, pepper and salt to taste.

6. Place the mushroom into a steamer & let steam until tender, for 20 minutes. Remove the

mushroom from steamer & slice into thin strips.
Serve it with the cooked pork chops.

For Roasted Red Pepper

1. Lightly rub the olive oil over the surface of the red pepper skin completely. Place the pepper completely on an open flame & roast for a couple of minutes, until the skin turns black.

2. Remove the pepper from flame & using a towel; rub the charred skin. Once removed, slice the pepper into thin strips & serve with the cooked pork chops.

BRAISED COLLARD GREENS WITH SMOKED PORK

TOTAL PREPARATION & COOKING TIME: 1 HOUR & 10 MINUTES
TOTAL SERVINGS: 10

INGREDIENTS

- 4 cups pork broth
- 1 cup pulled pork
- 6 pounds collard greens, fresh, tough ribs and stalks removed, roughly torn the leaves into bite-sized pieces
- 1 cup tarragon vinegar
- ½ yellow onion, sliced thinly
- 1 cup dark brown sugar, packed

COOKING DIRECTIONS

1. Add collard greens together with vinegar, sugar, pulled pork, onion, 1-gallon cold water and pork broth to a stock pot.

2. Bring everything together to a rolling boil, preferably over high heat settings and then decrease the heat settings to medium-low; let simmer for 45 minutes to an hour, until the greens are tender and very soft.

3. Divide the collards among bowls using tongs or a large-sized slotted spoon. Serve hot & enjoy.

VIETNAMESE GRILLED SMOKED PORK

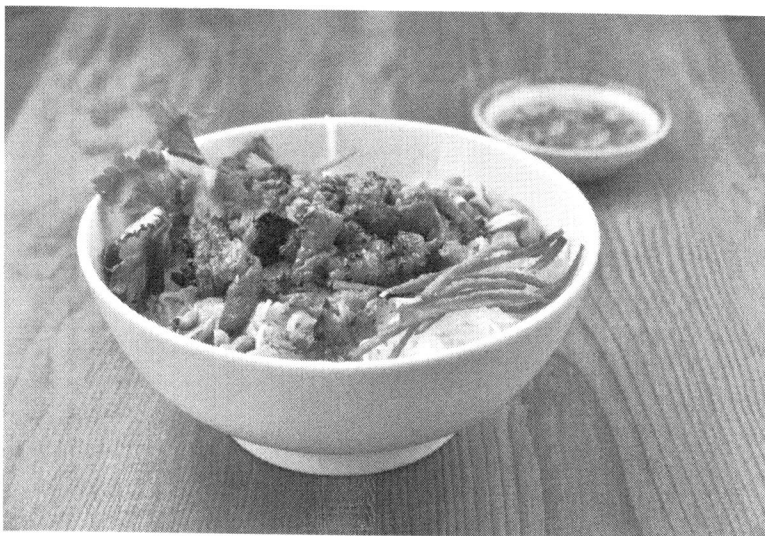

TOTAL PREPARATION & COOKING TIME: 1 HOUR & 30 MINUTES

TOTAL SERVINGS: 4

INGREDIENTS

- 2 bone-in pork chops, smoked, 1" thick (approximately 1 ½ pounds)
- 3 to 4 tbsp. fish sauce
- 5 tbsp. granulated sugar
- 1 carrot, large, peeled & grated (approximately 2 cups)
- 4 garlic cloves, minced
- ½ cup cilantro leaves, fresh & chopped roughly
- Juice & zest of 2 limes
- 2 tbsp. vegetable oil
- 3 tbsp. rice wine vinegar

- Red pepper flakes, crushed
- 4 cups long grain rice, cooked, warm
- Kosher salt to taste

COOKING DIRECTIONS

1. Whisk the rice wine vinegar together with 1 tbsp. of sugar in a large-sized mixing bowl for a couple of minutes, until the sugar is completely dissolved. Add the grated carrot; stir until the carrot is evenly combined. Season with salt to taste; set aside.

2. In a small-sized saucepan; combine the leftover sugar with ¼ cup of water. Bring it to a simmer for a couple of minutes, until the sugar is dissolved, over medium heat settings. Turn the heat off & add the fish sauce together with garlic, juice, and zest of lime and red pepper flakes (preferably a pinch or two). Spoon ¼ cup of the sauce out to baste the pork chops; reserve the remaining to serve with the rice bowls.

3. Heat a large-sized cast-iron grill or an outdoor grill over medium-high heat settings. Whisk the 1/4 cup of sauce together with oil and liberally brush the pork chops with the mixture, preferably all sides. Arrange the coated pork chops on the hot grill & cook for 5 minutes, until the pork is charred on both sides and warmed through.

4. Gently pull the pork away using a pair of tongs. Transfer to a large-sized cutting board & let rest for a couple of minutes. Cut off the bone of each pork chop & slice it thinly against the grain.

5. Divide the rice evenly among 4 bowls, preferably large sized. Toss the carrots with the cilantro. Top each bowl with a few pork slices; dividing the carrot salad evenly among the bowls & top with the leftover sauce. Give everything a good stir until evenly combined. Serve & enjoy.

INFORMATION ABOUT SMOKING MEAT

DIFFERENCE BETWEEN COLD AND HOT SMOKING

Depending on the type of grill that you are using, you might be able to get the option to go for a Hot Smoking Method or a Cold Smoking One. The primary fact about these three different cooking techniques which you should keep in mind are as follows:

1. **Hot Smoking:** In this technique, the food will use both the heat on your grill and the smoke to prepare your food. This method is most suitable for items such as chicken, lamb, brisket etc.

2. **Cold Smoking:** In this method, you are going to smoke your meat at a very low temperature such as 30 degree Celsius, making sure that it doesn't come into the direct contact with the heat. This is mostly used as a means to preserve meat and extend their life on the shelf.

3. **Roasting Smoke:** This is also known as Smoke Baking. This process is essentially a combined form of both roasting and baking and can be

performed in any type of smoker with a capacity of reaching temperatures above 82 degree Celsius.

By now you must be really curious to know about the different types of Smokers that are out there right?

Well, in the next section I am exactly going to discuss that!

THE DIFFERENT TYPES OF SMOKERS

Essentially, what you should know is that right now in the market, you are going to get three different types of Smokers.

CHARCOAL SMOKER

These types of smokers are hands down the best one for infusing the perfect Smoky flavor to your meat. But be warned, though, that these smokers are a little bit difficult to master as the method of regulating temperature is a little bit difficult when compared to normal Gas or Electric smokers.

ELECTRIC SMOKER

After the charcoal smoker, next comes perhaps the simpler option, Electric Smokers. These are easy to use and plug and play type. All you need to do is just plug in, set the temperature and go about your daily life. The smoker will do the rest. However, keep in mind that the finishing smoky flavor won't be as intense as the Charcoal one.

GAS SMOKERS

Finally, comes the Gas Smokers. These have a fairly easy mechanism for temperature control and are powered usually by LP Gas. The drawback of these Smokers is that you are going to have to keep checking up on your Smoker every now and then to ensure that it has not run out of Gas.

Now, these have been further dissected into different styles of the smoker. Each of which is preferred by Smokers of different experiences.

THE DIFFERENT STYLES OF SMOKERS

VERTICAL (BULLET STYLE USING CHARCOAL)

These are usually low-cost solutions and are perfect for first-time smokers.

VERTICAL (CABINET STYLE)

These Smokers come with a square shaped design with cabinets and drawers/trays for easy accessibility. These cookers also come with a water tray and a designated wood chips box as well.

OFFSET

These type of smokers have dedicated fireboxes that are attached to the side of the main grill. The smoke and heat required for these are generated from the firebox itself which is then passed through the main chamber and out through a nicely placed chimney.

KAMADO JOE

And finally, we have the Kamado Joe which is ceramic smokers are largely regarded as being the "Jack Of All Trades". These smokers can be used as low and slow smokers, grills, hi or low-temperature ovens and so on. They have a very thick ceramic wall which allows it to hold heat better than any other type of smoker out there, requiring only a little amount of charcoal.

CHOOSE YOUR WOOD

You need to choose your wood carefully because the type of wood you will use affect greatly to the flavor and taste of the meat. Here are a few options for you:

- Maple: Maple has a smoky and sweet taste and goes well with pork or poultry

- Alder: Alder is sweet and light. Perfect for poultry and fish.

- Apple: Apple has a mild and sweet flavor. Goes well with pork, fish, and poultry.

- Oak: Oak is great for slow cooking. Ideal for game, pork, beef, and lamb.

- Mesquite: Mesquite has a smoky flavor and extremely strong. Goes well with pork or beef.

- Hickory: Has a smoky and strong flavor. Goes well with beef and lamb.

- Cherry Has a mild and sweet flavor. Great for pork, beef, and turkey

THE DIFFERENT TYPES OF CHARCOAL

In General, there are essentially three different types of Charcoals. All of them are basically porous residues of black color that are made of carbon and ashes.

- **BBQ Briquettes:** These are the ones that are made from a fine blend of charcoal and char.
- **Charcoal Briquettes:** These are created by compressing charcoal and are made from sawdust or wood products.
- **Lump Charcoal:** These are made directly from hardwood and are the most premium quality charcoals available. They are completely natural and are free from any form of the additive.

FIND THE RIGHT
TEMPERATURE

- Start at 250F (120C): Start your smoker a bit hot. This extra heat gets the smoking process going.

- Temperature drop: Once you add the meat to the smoker, the temperature will drop, which is fine.

- Maintain the temperature. Monitor and maintain the temperature. Keep the temperature steady during the smoking process.

Avoid peeking every now and then. Smoke and heat two most important element make your meat taste great. If you open the cover every now and then you lose both of them and your meat loses flavor. Only the lid only when you truly need it.

CLEANLINESS OF THE MEAT

If you can make sure to follow the steps below, you will be able to ensure that your meat is safe from any kind of bacterial or airborne contamination.

This first step is very much essential as no market bought or freshly cut meat is completely sterile.

Following these, would greatly minimize the risk of getting affected by diseases.

- Make sure to properly wash your hands before beginning to process your meat. Use fresh tap water and soap/hand sanitizer.
- Make sure to remove any metal ornaments such as rings and watches from your wrist and hand before starting to handle the meat.
- Thoroughly clean the cutting surface using sanitizing liquid to remove any grease or unwanted contaminants. If you want to go for a homemade sanitizer, then you can simply make a solution of 1 part chlorine bleach and 10 parts water.
- The above-mentioned sanitizer should also be used to soak your tools such as knives and other equipment to ensure that they are safe to use as well.
- Alternatively, commercial acid based/ no rinsed sanitizer such as Star San will also work.
- After each and every use, all of the knives and other equipment such as meat grinders, slicers, extruders etc. should be cleaned thoroughly using soap water. The knives should be taken care in particular by cleaning the place just on top of the handle as it might contain blood and pieces of meat.

- When it comes to cleaning the surface, you should use cloths or sponges.

A note of sponges/clothes: It is ideal that you keep your sponge or cleaning cloth clean as it might result in cross-contamination. These are an ideal harboring place for foodborne pathogens. Just follow the simple steps to ensure that you are on the safe side:

- Make sure to clean your sponge daily. It is seen that the effectiveness of cleaning it increases if you microwave dam sponge for 1 minute and disinfect it using a solution of ¼ -1/2 teaspoon of concentrated bleach. This process will kill 99% of bacteria.
- Replace your sponge frequently as using the same sponge every single time (even with wash) will result in eventual bacterial growth.
- When not using the sponge, keep it in a dry place, making sure to wring it off of any loose food or debris.

KEEPING YOUR MEAT COLD

Mismanagement of temperature is one of the most common reasons for outbreaks of foodborne diseases. The study has shown that bacteria grow best at temperatures of 40 to 140 degree Fahrenheit/4-60 degree Celsius, which means that if not taken care properly, bacteria in the meat will start to multiply very quickly. The best way to prevent this from happening is to keep your meat cold before using it. Keep them eat in your fridge before processing them and make sure that the temperature is below 40 degrees Fahrenheit/4 degree Celsius.

KEEPING YOUR MEAT COVERED

All foods tend to start to diminish once they are opened from their packaging or exposed to air. However, the effect can be greatly minimized if you are able to cover or wrap the foods properly. Same goes for meat. Good ways of keeping your meat covered and wrapped include:

- Using aluminum foil to cover up your meat will help to protect it from light and oxygen and keep the moisture intact. However, since Aluminum is reactive, it is advised that a layer of plastic wrap is used underneath the aluminum foil to provide double protective layer.
- If keeping the meat in a bowl with no lid, then a plastic wrap can be used to seal the bowl providing an airtight enclosure.
- Re-sealable bags provide protection by storing it in a bag and squeezing out any air.
- Airtight glass or plastic containers with lids are good options as well.
- A type of paper known as Freezer paper is specifically designed to wrap foods that are to be kept in the fridge. These wraps are amazing for meat as well.
- Vacuum sealers are often used for Sous Vide packaging. These machines are a bit expensive but are able to provide excellent packaging by completely sucking out any air from a re-sealable bag. This greatly increases the meats shelf life both outside and in the fridge.

TOOLS AND EQUIPMENT

Knives: Sharp knives should be used to slice the meat accordingly. While using the knife, you should keep the following in mind.

- Always make sure to use a sharp knife
- Never hold a knife under your arm or leave it under a piece of meat
- Always keep your knives within visible distance
- Always keep your knife point down
- Always cut down towards the cutting surface and away from your body
- Never allow children to toy with knives unattended
- Wash the knives while cutting different types of food

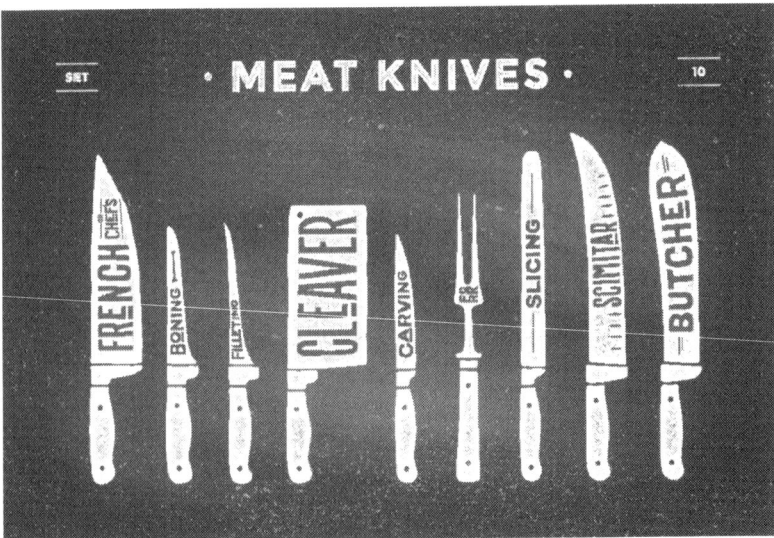

Mesh glove for protection: Cutting
the meat requires precision as you will be using a very sharp knife. The following types of the glove should be kept in mind:
- **Rubber gloves**
- **Butchering Gloves**
- **Mesh Glove**

Internal Thermometer: A meat
thermometer will help you to measure the internal temperature of the smoked meat to ensure that you are able to ensure that the meat is ready.

A NOTE ON CURING MEAT

The art of curing meat has been around since the ancient days! Simply put, this is a process through which meats are preserved for a really long time without the use of any harmful chemicals. All you need for the process are salt, nitrites and most importantly, a lot of time! Over time, the meat that you are processing will turn from a water packed and pliable piece to a stiff and dry meat with deliciously infused flavors. Generally speaking, dry cured meat is often said to pack a very soul touching Umami-flavor that tends to be both enlightening and mouthwatering. Interested to know the process? Well, the basic procedure of curing meat goes as follows!

Step 1: Decide the meat that you are going to cure. Most preferred parts include Pork loin and belly, brisket, beef hindquarter, mutton legs and duck breast.

Step 2: Trim off any excess fat, meat or tendons that might be hanging from your meat.

Step 3: If you have large sized meat, then try using a prong and stabbing it to ensure that you get better salt coverage. Make sure to do this just before applying your rub.

Step 4: Decide the kind of cure that you are going to use (the rub) and prepare the mixture accordingly.

Step 5: A general cure mixture would have a ratio of 2:1000 sodium nitrate and salt. This essentially means that you are to add 1000g of salt for every 2 grams of sodium nitrite. Make the mixture accordingly.

Step 6: Add any spices to the curing mixture if required. Some include:
- Peppercorns
- Sugar
- Coriander
- Star Anise
- Fennel Seed
- Citrus Zest

Step 7: Rub the mixture all over your meat using your hand. Make sure that the whole meat is covered properly.

As a precaution, make sure to not use metal trays (or even if you do use metal trays, use parchment paper).

Step 8: Allow the meat to refrigerate in your fridge for about 7-10 days depending on the size of your meat. Keep a small part of the meat uncovered to allow for proper air flow.

Step 9: Remove the meat from the fridge and wash it under cold water to ensure that you are able to remove as much of the rub as possible.

Step 10: Roll up the meat and tightly wrap it up in cheesecloth!

Step 11: Your cured meat is ready! Label it and hang it in a cool and dark place. It can be kept for about 2 weeks to 2 months. A cool walk-in refrigerator is ideal, which provides temperatures of 70 degrees Fahrenheit/21 degree Celsius

Step 12: Serve by removing cheesecloth and slicing it up.

CONCLUSION

I can't express how honored I am to think that you found my book interesting and informative enough to read it all through to the end. I thank you again for purchasing this book and I hope that you had as much fun reading it as I had writing it. I bid you farewell and encourage you to move forward and find your true Smoked Pork spirit!

P.S. Thank you for reading this book. If you've enjoyed this book, please don't shy, drop me a line, leave a review or both on Amazon. I love reading reviews and your opinion is extremely important for me.

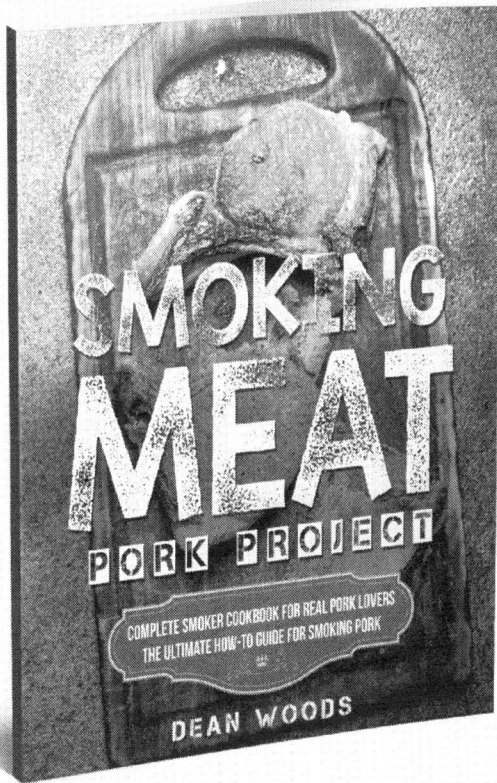

guarantee its accuracy and validity and cannot be held liable for any errors and/or omissions. Further, changes are periodically made to this book as and when needed. Where appropriate and/or necessary, you must consult a professional (including but not limited to your doctor, attorney, financial advisor or such other professional advisor) before using any of the suggested remedies, techniques, or information in this book.Upon using the contents and information contained in this book, you agree to hold harmless the Author from and against any damages, costs, and expenses, including any legal fees potentially resulting from the application of any of the information provided by this book. This disclaimer applies to any loss, damages or injury caused by the use and application, whether directly or indirectly, of any advice or information presented, whether for breach of contract, tort, negligence, personal injury, criminal intent, or under any other cause of action.

You agree to accept all risks of using the information presented in this book.

You agree that by continuing to read this book, where appropriate and/or necessary, you shall consult a professional (including but not limited to your doctor, attorney, or financial advisor or such other advisor as needed) before using any of the suggested remedies, techniques, or information in this book.

Made in the USA
Columbia, SC
10 December 2017